Motivation in 7 Simple Steps

Get Excited, Stay Motivated, Achieve Any Goal, and Create an Incredible Lifestyle

By Marta Tuchowska

by Marta Tuchowska

Introduction – Do You Want to Get on Motivational Fire and Be Unstoppable? The differences between "wishers" and "achievers"

So here you are, my friend. You wish to achieve big things, or just want to get some simple things done and keep moving forward. However, it always seems that those things are not for you. Maybe it wasn't the right time, the right place, or something happens to prevent you from achieving your goals. Maybe something even prevents you from setting your goals and realizing what it is that you want.

How many times have you been there? This, my friend, is called the World of Excuses. Here is one thing to understand—we have all been there. The difference between successful and unsuccessful people is that those who are successful or want to be successful make a conscious decision never to go back to the World of Excuses. They just know that it's not a place for them to hang out. It's like a party they don't want to be at. Now, what about you? Do you wish to continue your travels in the World of Excuses?

Of course, even successful people may sometimes end up in the World of Excuses. But they know some swift and powerful ways to transport themselves back to the World of Unlimited Motivation, Productivity, and Successful Habits. They have no choice. It's just who they are.

After going through this program, you won't have a choice either. You see, I am about to brainwash you and kick your ass—all in a good way, trust me. Even if you hate me at first, eventually, you will love me for it! This will be "positive brainwashing."

Aside from the World of Excuses or Party of Excuse Lovers, there are many other worlds or parties that you don't want to travel to. Let's face it—we are adults, not kids. We go to real parties, not kids' parties, right?

Do you want to end up in the World of Laziness, Negative Thinking, Naysaying, Unhealthy Habits, and finally Anxiety? Yes, very often, lack of action leads to anxious states. Deep inside, you know you should be doing YOUR STUFF—your Sacred Stuff that makes you the NEW, SUCCESSFUL you.

I have a question for you. You need to be honest with yourself. Everyone is welcome here; I only ask one simple question to make a selection. You see, I want to ensure that this program ends up only in the hands of the right people. I don't want my work to end up in the hands of haters and those who would rather spend their time questioning other people's efforts and success rather than learning from them.

Here's the question.

Do you want to be successful?

Let me ask you again...

Do you want to be successful?

The answer should be HECK yeah. If you are not too sure, ask yourself WHY NOT.

First of all, people have different definitions of success. I am cool with that. Everyone is different, which is the beauty of life. But certain things—like mindset, for example—are always the same. Those things will remain the same for the next 100 years, 200 years, and even 100,000 years from now.

You see, success is about achieving your goals—your OWN goals, not someone else's. This is important because in this program, we will focus on your internal motivation, and we will try to light your inner fire. For both of us to be more successful, you need to be honest with yourself.

By the way, I say "for us to be more successful" because my goal is to help you become successful. That is my definition of success, and that is what has driven me to create this program. I want to help you achieve your personal goals.

You probably know that there are two kinds of motivation: internal and external. External motivation drives most people. They get up in the morning (usually with an alarm clock they hate), get ready for work, drive to work, and then work. When they get back home, they go grocery shopping (because there is no food in the fridge). Now, there is nothing wrong with external motivation—that is when we do things that we have to do. Most people (unless they suffer from some mental disorders) don't have a problem with that. Going to work is automatic. It has to be done. Showering is automatic; it has to be done. As I said before, these actions are automatic for most of us, but some people—for example, the severely depressed—might even have problems with that.

The bottom line is that most of us do things as they have to be done, so we, therefore, work with external motivation. However, it's when you start unleashing your inner motivation that amazing things are going to happen.

Getting up super early and reading a book or going for a run at 5 A.M. on our own accord can be a challenge for most people. But these actions can add to our personal development and help us to grow as human beings.

Personally, I feel much more proud and fulfilled about things that I decide to do myself. I had to figure out the whole process myself because I wanted to achieve my goals. But most people do things that they are told to do either by their bosses, family, or society in general. When the time comes to choose to do something for themselves and take massive action on that decision, they say that they are not motivated! How sad is that?

How can one not feel motivated to do things that will help them grow and become stronger? How is that possible that human beings have no problem taking action on doing something that may help other people be more successful, but they forget about their own success?

Most people would say that they are not motivated to:

- Eat healthier and work out;
- Pursue their passion, change their career, or start a business;
- Change their habits and get rid of limiting beliefs to create more happiness and zest for life;

— Start a new relationship even if they have been hurt before.

But if you keep asking them, they would probably want to:

— Have a healthy, sexy body, physical fitness, and lots of energy;
— Do something that they love and make a good income while pursuing their passion;
— Create a life full of happiness and abundance;
— Have awesome relationships and feel loved and supported.

The problem that many people have is that just by saying "I am not motivated to…" they reject the incredible life that is waiting for them. They also don't recognize the fact that they can create their life and that it's always those small things and small decisions that can significantly impact their lives.

Think about yourself. Think about three little things that you could be doing every day and how those little things could compound into big things. One thing is sure: five years from now, you will get somewhere. The question is: where? Is that going to be a place that you want to get to? Or maybe a place where you don't want to end up? Are you aware of the responsibility that your actions have on not only your own life but on those around you? Are you willing to be more and more responsible every day?

Where do you see yourself one year from now? What about five years from now? Picture your ideal life and your perfect day. Let's say it's Monday or Tuesday, just a "regular weekday," but in your new, better life. Travel to the future. What do you want to achieve five years from now? Where do you want to live? What kind of body do you want to create? How much money do you want to make? What career or business do you want? Do you want to be married or single? With or without kids? Picture it all now.

Let's do an exercise. Take a piece of paper and start writing it down. Start with:

- *It's Monday morning. I get up at [add your ideal wake-up time].*

- Describe your perfect house. Who do you live with? What do you have for breakfast? What kinds of clothes are you going to wear? Where do you work? Maybe you work from home? Or perhaps you are a traveler? Be specific.

- Write it all down. There are no boundaries. The purpose of this exercise is to feel the power that you have to create your life thanks to achieving your goals. It will also help you forget the phrase *"but I am not motivated to..."* I am deleting it from your vocabulary from now on.

How can you not be motivated to have an excellent life? Nobody else will do it for you. You need to accept it. It's you, your mindset, and your actions. This book focuses on squeezing out the best motivational juices from the fruits that you are growing in the back garden of your mindset right now. You started your motivational garden by taking an interest in this book. Maybe you even started it before that. Perhaps you already understand the connection between motivation, responsibility, taking action, thinking like an achiever, and lifestyle creation. Maybe you are reading this book to reinforce your habits and check out my viewpoint on this fascinating topic. Again, I welcome you all. As long as you want to be successful, keep reading.

In this day and age, we have it so easy. We don't need to fight or struggle like our ancestors had to (even to satisfy their basic needs like finding some food). Many people become conformists and begin living like robots. There is an excellent comparison that Tony Robbins uses called living a *box life*. You get up (in a box that is your house or apartment), and you have a box breakfast. You get in a box (a car), and you move to another box (your office). After this set of box rituals, you go back home (in a box) and watch a box while eating some boxed food.

I think this box comparison is just brilliant. I love Tony Robbins, by the way. All his motivational speeches help me get even more motivated and committed to my goals.

By picking up this program, you have decided to work on your internal motivation and get much more done than most people who choose to lead a "boxed lifestyle."

You want to be and think outside the box, right? Whenever you see people achieving some amazing things, it's not because "they just got lucky." It's because they worked on their inner motivation. Your internal motivation is like a muscle. It needs to be well taken care of. You need to grow it, stretch it, feed it, and even treat it to massages now and then. Every motivational book or program you go through is a like a little massage for your internal motivation muscles. It will help them release tension and work much better for you.

This is why you need to focus on yourself. You need to focus on your inner motivation. Most people are too busy achieving someone else's goals. These may be the goals for their company, spouse, parents, or just general "fit into society" stuff. Now, I am not saying that trying to fit in is wrong, just like trying to stand out isn't wrong. You need to follow your voice and intuition.

Everyone is different. Again, you need to feel your energy first. You need to reconnect with yourself. The tools and strategies that I am about to share with you can be applied to all areas of your life. They can help you achieve your health and fitness goals, self-growth goals, business goals, career goals, and even some personal and lifestyle goals. Life isn't just about work, even if you love it, right?

Motivation can be not only learned, but mastered. This is the number one tip I am giving you. Forget about the concept of naturally motivated people. You see, motivation is always natural. It cannot be artificial.

Here is one crucial thing to understand, and you may also realize that this was something that was holding you back. Yep, it is kind of a limiting factor for many of us—it even used to be one for me.

You go on Facebook and browse through the "news." You see some of your friends and acquaintances achieving their goals and embracing success. You see people creating businesses, people falling in love and having awesome relationships, people traveling, and people changing things and just being active and busy with their exciting agendas. And you are still stuck there with the same old mindset. Then you conclude, "I am not motivated. All those people achieve things because they are so motivated and driven and I am not. I guess that's just the way it is."

End of story. Adios. Ciao. You have just made friends with your limiting belief. You said that other people are naturally motivated and you are not. You are just about to get on a plane to the World of Excuses. Ouch.

How about getting a last minute flight to the World of Motivation and Positive Thinking?

Can you understand this negative pattern? Now, I am not here to judge you or anything. I have been there myself. Six years ago, I felt the same. I saw other people achieving their goals (health, travel, jobs, and relationships), and I felt stuck. It was only when I realized that the problem was me that I was finally able to focus on finding the solutions.

Again, I am not preaching. This is why I like using some examples from my own life. It's not always easy. I know that there will be many people going through this program. I am also exposing some of my weaknesses and past failures here, but I am not ashamed to be transparent as I know it will help other people. It can inspire them. I want to show you and other individuals who go through this program that you can create something out of nothing. You can create your own way. You can hypnotize yourself.

OK, enough talking about me. This program is about you. You are the primary focus here; you are the hero. Now, maybe your situation is not as dramatic as what I have pictured above. Maybe it is not as dramatic as a Facebook user who is just about to say adios to his or her success, assuming that it's not for them and that it's only for their friends who "got lucky."

Maybe you are on the right track and just want to master a few new tricks. Or maybe you have got some awesome things done and decided to start this program. Maybe it's just because you resonated with me in some way, or you were curious. Something made you join this program.

Just one thing I need to repeat: If you don't want to be successful, this stuff is not for you. I don't want to waste your time. I am limiting this program only to the tiny percentage of people who want to be successful.

If this makes you confused and you are of two minds, I will venture to say that you are on the right track. Let me tell you this (and I am sure it will motivate you): Very few people decide to invest their time in reading and researching. Very few people choose to work on their mindset and motivation. I would even say that it's easier to find people working on their bodies rather than their minds. You see, my friend, working on your mind can be a journey. Sometimes there is a dark side to it. You need to face your fears and limiting beliefs. But the final reward is a new, stronger version of yourself. You develop your mental and emotional muscles.

With stronger mental and emotional muscles, you can do anything, go anywhere in your life, and reach any goal. By the way, if your objective is to create a sexy, fit body and be in the gym every day, guess what—you also need the right mindset. I have noticed that many fitness people have subconsciously mastered this mindset. They developed habits and discipline, and they can utilize them as their tools for other goals like studying, creating businesses, and even personal goals.

Here is the essence of this chapter:

1. Motivation can be learned and mastered. If you don't agree, that means that you are cultivating a limiting belief which only takes your success away.

2. Forget about the concept of "naturally motivated" people. Everyone can be naturally motivated. Those who get motivated, stick to what they do, finally create new powerful habits, and achieve their goals are all people who used certain mind tricks and techniques that you are about to learn. Some of them may have used those techniques subconsciously; it doesn't matter. They used them, and as a result, they had a set of rituals that would help them move forward.

3. There are two kinds of motivation—external and internal. In this program, we are going to focus on your internal motivation, something that comes from within you and is in alignment with your real desires and life goals. Something that will help you and will guide you on the journey of achieving all kinds of successes in different areas of your life.

Free Bonus for More Motivation

Before we get into our 7 steps, I would like to offer you a free gift. It's a 5 day motivation challenge + free audio (recorded by myself so that you know who's talking to you in this book) to help you get and stay motivated. During the challenge, you will receive 5 super powerful motivational tips via email (1 tip a day- Marta will be in your inbox to make sure you move forward) to help you transform your life the way you have always wanted. Oh and the motivational audio is an added bonus, just because I felt super motivated (and I like spoiling you).

Visit my website at:

www.LifestyleDesignSuccess.com/motivation

And join the free challenge now. No worries, no spam. Only cool stuff.

Be in that 5% of people who actually take action!

Chapter 1
Step 1 – Excuses. Make Sure You Get Rid of Them

Some people feel like they want to change something, but deep inside, they are full of excuses and limiting beliefs that prevent them from taking action. I am not judging or anything because I have always been guilty of that myself. I don't even think that "guilty" is the right word. I have also been a victim of the World of Excuses.

The worst thing that you can do is indulge in excuses or even other "proof" that there is no point in taking action because *it won't work, it's a scam,* or it's *"not for you."* Sometimes, you may be doing this subconsciously. Your brain is trying to protect you from taking action. After all, the function of your brain is to make sure you survive. The question is: Do you just want to survive, or do you want to live? Are all those excuses coming up because deep inside you fear that you might fail?

My guess is that, if you picked up this program, you want to live, and even more than that. You want to achieve things, and you want to be an example to other people, right? Think about it. Think about how good it will feel to create an example for your family, friends, and children.

Now, back to excuses. I have noticed both from my own experience as well as from observing some of my students and readers that, very often, we have this mechanism that tries to protect us from changes and anything that is new— even creating a healthier lifestyle or thinking differently. Of course, deep inside, we need a system that protects us from bad decisions. But more often than not, this mechanism does us more harm than good. It prevents us from taking action, and as a result, we may reject something even before we have tried it!

Let me give you an example. I have recently created and published a course on the alkaline/ plant based inspired diet. Well, not just a diet, but a general lifestyle change. I added many motivational tools and techniques, and I also listed all the possible obstacles that can prevent people from achieving their health and fitness goals.

While most of my students decided to trust me and follow through and focus on the practical side of the course (lifestyle, recipes, and relaxation), there were also a couple of individuals who decided to question everything. They did not even complete the course. After the first lesson, they decided to go online and look for some articles that put down plant based diets and living a healthy lifestyle in general.

I advised them to relax and try it for themselves. Honestly, at first, I was a bit angry, but then I decided to let it go. I realized that they were all victims of certain negative patterns, and quite frankly, at some point in my life, I had been there as well. This is a dark place of self-doubt. You are too scared to try new things because deep inside you think you may fail. This is why you try to come up with as many excuses as you possibly can.

Do any of these lines ring a bell?

- "What's the point of studying and educating myself if there are no jobs and starting a business is only for the rich guys?"

- "What's the point of eating a healthy diet if I always put on weight anyway?"

- "What's the point of starting a new relationship if real love does not exist?"

- "What's the point of moving to another country if I can't speak the language?"

- "What's the point of changing my job if I may get fired anyway?"

- "What's the point of starting my own business if most businesses don't even survive five years?"

Again, we need to make sure we get rid of all those disempowering beliefs. These are like weeds that need to be removed to create more space in our motivational garden.

Imagine you want to learn a foreign language. Let's say you want to learn French. You hire a teacher, and instead of commencing your journey of studying and practicing French, you search for cases of people who failed or did not follow through as they should have. Or you might look for research that shows, after a certain age, it's hard to learn a foreign language. All of these actions are creating excuses and making you feel paralyzed rather than feeling empowered and taking massive action.

Let's go through a few more disempowering beliefs and lines:

- "What's the point of trying this healthy lifestyle if there are tons of articles saying that this whole alkaline pH thing is a big bunch of BS?"

Answer: Well, maybe you should focus on people who are living this lifestyle and are getting excellent health results. It's easy to fabricate an article, but it's harder to create a healthy lifestyle that inspires others. What are you going to stick to? Do you want to become a hater and reject your goals before you start?

-"What's the point of learning a foreign language if I can just use Google translator? Besides, at my age, I will never master the grammar perfectly, and I will always have a weird accent. It's not for me!"

Answer: So what? Who cares? There is nothing wrong with speaking or writing a language as a second language. Think about all of the new people you can meet! You can still achieve the native-like or fluent proficiency, and an accent is always sexy and unique. Focus on people who got committed to learning new languages and got great results. They will help you while the naysayers and haters will only make you travel back to the World of Excuses.

Now, let's dig deeper. You need to face your fear and analyze it. We all have fears. I have fears, obsessions, and bad habits, but a while back, I got committed to fighting them and moving forward. All I want to do is to move forward. I am not perfect, and I am not a self-help or spiritual guru. I am a human being, just like you. We are different, yet we are similar. I am here to share not only my successes but also my failures so that hopefully I can make your path to success easier and more fun.

What are your fears? What stops you from taking action? What if I told you that there is always a solution and that you can always find some good in the negative?

Here is the most typical fear that prevents people from taking action:

-I might fail. So what? The most successful people failed dozens of times before they succeeded. To me, real failure is when you don't take action. If you don't say anything, you don't move. It's like you don't exist and don't live your life. We live only once. Do you want to live a life full of fear and excuses?

My Tip

You need to develop an entrepreneurial mindset. Now, I am not saying that you need to start your own business or something. To me, entrepreneurship, in a metaphorical way, is simply *a state of mind.* It doesn't matter if you work for someone or not. Some people may have a business, but they lack the entrepreneurial mindset that I am just about to explain. Some people have jobs and are employed, yet they manage to develop this *entrepreneurial mindset.*

This is a metaphor, so don't take it directly. Read with an open mind. I always make it clear that there is nothing wrong with working for someone else. I have never said that a

24

person who is running a business is better than an individual who is employed. Both are awesome. People make different choices. The most important thing is to know what works for you.

When I say "entrepreneurial mindset," I refer to a kind of person who is committed to taking action. They focus on the process and don't get fixated on the final results and possible setbacks ("What will happen if I fail?"). They know that failure also leads to success.

"In order to double your level of success, you must also double your level of failure." – Darren Jacklin (Motivational speaker, angel investor, and corporate trainer)

I used to be a fan of this limiting belief. It would make my life comfortable for a short period when I was just hiding my head in a shell, like a proverbial turtle:

"Try once (maybe twice), if you fail, it's not for you. Forget about it."

I would use it as an excuse. I would also take "advice" from others who would just say:

- *"You are not talented enough."*

- *"You are not confident enough."*

- *"You are not tall enough."*

- *"You don't have enough physical strength."*

- *"What, you want to start a business? First you need to go to a university and study something like sales and marketing."*

- *"You cannot write a book. English is your second language; you are going to suck at it. Besides, who reads books today?"*

- *"You can't create an athletic body; you are a weakling. Why even bother?"*

Sound familiar?

You need to start applying the mindset of an explorer and entrepreneur. Or even a mindset of an immigrant. They have to make it happen. They take the risk. They leave their country, and all they have is a dream, ambition, drive, and commitment. This is the recipe for success.

Here are your new friends:

- *"Don't give up."*

- *"Never accept no for an answer."*

- *"Keep asking. To every question you don't ask, the answer is always no."*

- *"Accept failure as a part of success."*

- *"Whatever it is that you do, do it for yourself. Reject all of those naysayers."*

- *"Focus on people who have walked the path of positivity and use them as your mentors and role models."*

- *"Don't reject anything before you have tried it."*

- *"Failure is when you don't even try to take action and make it happen."*

- *"Motivation is about making a conscious decision to live a life that you want!"*

Why do we have fears that can prevent us from taking action?

It's straightforward; just think about it. Maybe you failed in the past. Or you tried to learn something new, but the first lesson was painful. Maybe you were doing well, but you came across a hater who wanted to belittle your success, and you did not feel secure enough to carry on. Maybe you did not get enough support from your loved ones.

Whatever it was, accept it. Focus on the now. I believe in you. I believe in you because you want to read, learn, grow, and change something.

This book is like having coffee with me. I am not here to preach. I want to be your friend who encourages you, shares her own experiences, and sometimes kicks your ass (but in a good way). I know that some people need to get their asses kicked to take action while other people need some gentle words of encouragement and someone to gently hold their hand and walk them through the process. I can do both.

Let's carry on.

You need to make a decision that you will never settle for less than you can be, do, or have. You know I believe in you, and now you need to believe in yourself. If you give up even before you start, or you look for excuses and pseudo-proof to justify your decision to quit, it means that your brain is trying to protect you.

You need to go back to the past and face it. See your old self doing things in a certain way and say bye-bye, adios, ciao. Don't hate yourself from back then. Please don't hate yourself. You need to develop self-love and self-empathy. So have a conversation with yourself from the past.

Say to your old self:

"Even though I don't agree with your actions from the past, I respect you and I love you. It's thanks to you that I am now driven to take massive action and work on my internal motivation, which will take my entire life to a whole new level. I am now an achiever!"

Write it down. Modify it if you want. Keep it right in front of you every day, as much as you can. Now there is no turning back. You have accepted the fact that this will be a journey. There will be peaks and valleys, ups and downs. But if you stay where you were before, the World of Excuses, there will only be downs.

You have two choices:

1. Live a life of progress and acceptance, of peaks and valleys. As you move forward, there are more ups than downs.
2. Live a life of regret and fear and have no chance to transform it.

Which pill do you wish to take? The red one, or the blue one? Now, I am sure you have taken the first one. Good job. It will give you a nice, natural high, you will see!

Now, we need to reinforce your new beliefs. Let's go through this short exercise together. In this exercise, you will ask yourself some questions. It's like self-coaching and evaluation. Think about a goal from the past where you failed to take action and just came up with a bunch of excuses.

- What was it? When was it?

- How could this have been avoided?

- What can you do today to think and do things differently?

How have those experiences made you stronger? What have you learned from them? Trust me, focusing on the bright side helps a lot. No matter how bad the situation, there is always a bright side.

Can you use this experience as a motivator? If not, why not? Are there any other experiences from your life (or maybe the lives of those around you) where you did not even take action to begin with?

What are you going to do now to help you get rid of excuses and limiting beliefs?

Here's what we have learned in this chapter:

- Many of us don't take action because we are scared of pain, rejection, and failure as well as judgment and "what if" patterns. You need to give yourself freedom and space to fail. You need to accept the fact that there will be peaks and valleys. You need to embrace the fact that taking action will help you strengthen your emotional muscles, and gradually, taking action will be much easier.

- If you go through the process of working on your motivation and taking action toward your goals, you will master the success mindset (I call it the Entrepreneurial Mindset, and it does not mean you need to have your own business), which will be the number one tool in your success toolbox. It will help you achieve even more of your goals. And the more you achieve, the easier it becomes. The more you achieve, the more motivated you feel.

- You can use your past failures as your motivators in the present.

Chapter 2
Step 2 – Travel Back to the Past and Make Friends with Your Emotions

While going through this chapter, I want you to relax. Take a few deep breaths, stretch, grab yourself a cup of herbal infusion, and if you want, put on some relaxing music. I know that you will be much more successful with this step (as well as all the others) if you go through it while feeling relaxed and peaceful. If something happened today and you feel out of balance, it may be a good idea to have a break from this program and focus on yourself and relax first. It's just my tip; the final decision is entirely up to you.

In this step, we are going to travel back to the past and celebrate both your successes and achievements as well as failures. Yes, when treated in the right way, even failures can help us be successful. It's just our modern, fast-paced society that only celebrates instant victory and success. However, when you think about it, failing is not a bad thing. If you failed at something, it means that at least you took some action and were committed. That is so much better than not doing or saying anything, not taking action, and choosing just to be quiet, and therefore, not fail.

As Darren Jacklin says, "Success is a well-managed failure." I love this line. It's beautiful and inspiring.

It may be hard to ingrain this mindset at first, primarily because of the above-mentioned social conditioning where you either win, or you don't. However, we must also be aware of the process of achieving our goals. This process consists of baby steps, and very often, failure is just one of those steps. It forms part of a much bigger picture.

So from now on, I don't want to hear any excuses like, "Yeah, I tried that before, but wasn't good at it." If you find yourself bringing up your past failures and using them as excuses, you need to go back to the previous step.

Now let's travel to the past. Think about at least three big things that you have achieved. Something that made you feel proud of yourself. I am sure there must be some significant achievements in your life. You may even go back to your childhood or teenage years. How did it feel to learn to ride a bicycle or swim? How did it feel to get your driver's license? What about your personal life—how did it feel to get a date with someone you liked? Even if it didn't work out, let's just focus on the emotions you felt when you achieved this dating goal.

Grab a piece of paper and write all your successes down. I can guarantee that eventually, you will come up with many more than three. It doesn't have to be big. You see, our modern society usually defines success as making tons of money. Of course, if you're after financial success, this definition makes sense. However, we want to unleash our inner motivation, which we can use to improve all areas of life, not just one. It is essential to learn how to talk to yourself, listen to yourself, and make friends with your feelings and emotions.

If you get stuck and can't think of anything, it means that you are getting blocked. You need to relax. Again, stretch and breathe. Listen to music that makes you feel good. Then start over again.

Let's say that many years ago you got accepted at a top-tier college or university. Maybe now you don't feel that proud of it. Perhaps you are thinking, "So what if other people don't have education and make more money than I do?" Again, this is the wrong approach. You are getting angry with yourself, and self-anger doesn't help. Think about how you felt about having success with your goal twenty years ago. Picture all of the details, how you called your family and threw a party to celebrate your success. How did it feel?

I will ask you again: How did you feel back then? How can those feelings help you now? Did you feel like everything was possible? Did you feel like you were unstoppable and wanted to do more and more?

Maybe one of your achievements from the past was to save up some money and travel abroad. Go back to the past. I am sure that while waiting for that plane to take off, you were thinking where to go next. You were buzzing!

What happened next? Why did you stop?

Here is very simple exercise for you to do. It consists of three simple steps.

1.Make sure you write down all your past achievements and always keep the list in your office, wallet, or somewhere you will see it often.

Always be proud of your past accomplishments. Of course, it's normal that, with time, our past achievements don't seem as significant anymore. A 60-year-old man usually won't go around bragging about getting a driver's license, right?

Here's the balance that we want to achieve. We want to be proud of our past achievements and use positive feelings and emotions from back then as our fuel and motivator. However, we also want to move forward and keep achieving more. We don't want to stop and rest on our laurels.

The challenge that many people usually have is that they either try to move on too fast and forget about their past achievements and focus too much on what they still don't have or the other way around. Some people live too much in the past and spend way too much time on being proud of what they used to be. Now, I believe that after completing this step, you will find your balance that will also result in emotional well-being. Don't be too strict on yourself, but don't be overindulgent, either.

2.Travel back to the past and, this time, focus on your failures. Write down what you did, what you wanted, and how you failed. You can use those experiences as motivators. A little bit of pain (or slightly more than that) can do wonders in your life. Just be honest with yourself. All you need to do is share your past failures with the most important person in your life, which is you. Yes, you!

What emotions and feelings did you experience with your past failures? What could have gone differently? Was achieving your goal dependent on other people? Was your failure because you did not work hard enough? Or you worked hard but were not able to focus your efforts in the right direction?

Talk to yourself from the past. Don't be angry with yourself. Stand in front of the mirror and just say: I have a vital message for you from ten years ago.

Carry on with something like:

I am not judging you; I respect you. I learned a lot from you. But now I am a new person. Now, I am an achiever. I don't quit just because I failed. I am not angry at you because it's thanks to you that I learned. It's thanks to you that I finally decided that I want to create a better, stronger, and more empowered version of myself. It's thanks to you that I finally said: Enough! It's time to move on.

3.Focus on what you learned from your previous experiences and turn your failures into your successes.

Travel back to the past, pick up at least one mega failure, and focus on the facts. How did this experience help you become a better person? What did you learn? What can you learn? How can this help you now?

For example:

I don't want to depend on other people. I need to learn how to organize my time. I need to learn to put on a thick skin so that I don't quit just because a few bitter haters are trying to diminish my success. I need to learn to take more care of my health and fitness so that I can focus and concentrate better. I need to avoid negative environments and create a group of positive, successful people that bring me closer to the entrepreneurial, motivational mindset.

What all highly motivated and successful people share is that they know how to remain calm in moments of hardship. They know how to turn negative into positive. I understand that some situations may be hard. I have been through lots of pain and rejection in my life. At that time, I heard many spiritual gurus telling me, "Look for good in bad and turn negative into positive," and it would just make me mad. However, I had to let it go. I had to learn to get rid of negativity and sarcasm and at least try to see good in bad.

I call this working on your Positive Muscle. At first, it may be hard. Don't give up. Carry on. Make sure you are at the Positive Gym every day and make your Positive Muscle grow big and powerful. After regular practice, your mind will be able to turn negative into positive almost effortlessly.

Key points you have learned in this step:

- Use past failures and successes and your motivators; learn what you can from them. Embrace the old feelings and emotions.
- Pain, rejection, and disappointment are negative emotions. However, you can also use them as assets. They will help you create an incredible set of motivational life tools for your VIP Positive Toolbox.
- Never stop being proud of your past successes, even the small ones. However, don't treat them as the end of your journey. It's only the beginning.

Chapter 3
Step 3 – Redefine Yourself, Love Yourself, and Cultivate Self-Acceptance

We have previously stated that many people quit before they start. Aside from every possible, and very often, made-up excuses, they may have certain limiting beliefs that are preventing them from taking action.

Limiting beliefs are like dirt accumulating in our minds (and it should be out of our motivational gardens, right?). The best "cure" is to try some "mental peeling" followed by a VIP Spa treatment for our mind. I am about to show you the simplest and most efficient way to get rid of our limiting beliefs. In fact, it's so simple that I know that you may even doubt if it works. If you catch yourself doing this, make sure you carry on with this chapter, even if you think it's weird or strange. We already know that successful people do certain things, and you are successful, right?

Of course, the first step is to recognize your limiting beliefs and understand their patterns, where they come from, and why we have them. We don't want to be slaves to our limiting beliefs.

When left untreated, limiting beliefs can not only manifest themselves in a bunch of excuses that we create to protect ourselves from potential failure or extra effort. They can also take our emotional wellness away and even turn us into haters.

Here's the essential thing to understand. Society has brainwashed us. We were taught that it's better, or safer, to be like everyone else and stay in the box or hide in proverbial shells. Think about your limiting beliefs. Maybe some of the most common limiting beliefs listed below ring a bell? Perhaps you currently have or have had some of them at some point in your life?

Examples of limiting beliefs that will kill your motivation, passion, and zest for life:

- All rich people are dishonest and greedy.

- In order to get super rich, you need a good college education, good contacts, and rich parents.

- Living a healthy lifestyle is boring and not fun.

- I hate drinking vegetable juices. They have no taste.

- Weekends are to have fun! Go out and drink.

- People who read self-help books must be messed up.

- What's the point of learning about motivation if you lose it eventually?

- Weight loss diets never work. All the healthy diet stuff is BS. If your genes are fat, you will always be fat. It doesn't matter what you eat.

- If you are born poor, you will always be poor.

- All men are the same! You can't trust them!

- All women are the same. They only want rich guys!

- What's the point of doing yoga to relax if I can just go for drinks with friends?

The truth is that we often get limiting beliefs from our family and friends as well as past experiences. For example, someone who suffered in love more than once may develop a limiting belief that all men or women "are all the same." Someone who has seen a dishonest person getting rich in an illegal way may immediately develop a limiting belief that all rich people "are the same."

How to stop being a victim of limiting beliefs?

It all comes down to what you decide to focus on from that moment on. If you want to become wealthy, yet you despise all the rich people you see around you, guess what? You will never reach your financial goals.

What you should focus on are positive role models. Of course, some rich people steal or lie, just like there are poorer people who also do the same. If you want to become a wealthy person and have financial success, your focus should be 100 percent on rags-to-riches stories. Read and listen to biographies and motivational stories. Learn more about self-made men, for example, Robert Herjavec. You can be a son of an immigrant factory worker but make a fortune. Finally, if you start reading more about self-made success stories, you will start noticing certain mindset patterns that will ultimately help you stretch and expand your overall mindset. That is what we want, right? We want to take care of our mental and emotional muscles.

Positive affirmations

You need to talk to yourself, and even if you already do, you need do it more. This is something that most people never do. But we have already stated that successful people do things that other (unsuccessful) people don't want to do, right? The best way to do it is create positive affirmations like for example:

- I create my destiny. I create my life.

- I increase my income every month.

- I love what I do, and I do what I love.

- I deserve to have more money because I want to take better care of my family, or even better, I make [put specific amount] dollars a month and I am proud of myself.

- I attract amazing business opportunities.

- I am full of ideas that I can monetize.

- I create products and services that help other people, or if you work for someone else, I help my bosses grow their business and I increase my income as well. I love my job!

Create positive affirmations. You may have different affirmations for different areas of life (health, finances, relationships, and lifestyle) or focus on just one area of life if that is your priority. Always look for testimonials and biographies of people who have already achieved what you want to achieve.

Here are some positive health and fitness affirmations:

- I use food as my fuel, not as a drug.

- What I eat helps me achieve my health and wellness goals.

- I love drinking vegetable juices; they give me so much energy.

- I take care of my body and it takes care of me.

- I am committed to learning more about health and fitness.

- I love life and life loves me!

- Moving my body makes me feel happy and proud of myself.

- I love my body and I am committed to working on it every day.

- I look great in my new fitness clothes.

Creating positive affirmations will help you communicate with your sub-conscious mind. Even though you may not realize it yet, eventually your subconscious mind will work for you. Besides, you will feel much more positive, motivated, and focused.

However, the key point of affirmations is to redefine yourself before you set your goals and explore motivational techniques. You need to prepare your mind, emotions, and soul. No amount of motivational coaching will help if you refuse to become your own coach. Say goodbye to your old self. Create a new, stronger version of your body and mind.

So, who are you now?

For example, if your goal is to create a healthy, fit body, your new definition of yourself could be:

- I am a health and fitness nut. I love trying out new workouts and healthy recipes. I love my healthy and fit body, and I make healthy choices. I am full of energy. My body is my temple.

- I am healthy and fit—it's just WHO I AM.

This is really powerful. Make sure you always add: "It's just who I am."

You see, a good writer writes every day, even if they don't feel like doing so. My friends usually get surprised when I tell them that I have a rigorous writing routine and that I am up at 5 – 6 A.M. already hard at work. It's because I want to make sure that my most productive working hours are spent on writing and creating content for my blog and courses. It wasn't always easy, especially in the winter, but I created a new definition of myself. This is who I am. I am an early riser. I love getting up early, and I don't want to oversleep my life. I want to be productive. I don't think I am a good writer as far as writing trade is concerned, but I know I can create quality content that helps other people. That is what motivated me. As an author and coach, I want to create extremely informative, motivational, and inspiring content. My definition of myself also creates responsibility.

What is your definition? What is your responsibility?

A good painter paints every day, even if they don't feel like doing it. It's just who they are. A good entrepreneur is always alert and looking for new business ideas. It's just who they are. A runner runs every day. Since I defined myself as a fitness nut, I work out every day. Of course, work out plans also include well designed rest days. Work smart, right? It just has to be done.

It's really powerful. Try it. Who are you?

If your main area of focus now is your relationship, you could redefine yourself that way:

> *I attract amazing people and circumstances in my life. However, I am also grateful for painful experiences as they help me get stronger and strengthen my emotional muscles.*

If you are pursuing higher education, going through a professional course, or some other process to change your

51

career, make sure you create your definition now. For example, a few years ago, I was committed to studying massage therapy and holistic nutrition. At that time, I was still at a job I hated. But deep inside, my definition of myself was: "I am a massage therapist and holistic nutritionist. I love my work!" Those two simple sentences helped me get through many obstacles and sacrifices I had to make to change my career.

If you study medicine, stand in front of a mirror and say to yourself:

I am a doctor. I love helping other people.

If you study engineering, say to yourself: I *am an engineer. This is why I do what I do.*

Repeat your affirmations and new definitions of yourself and your actions as much as you can. Employ your whole physiology. Feel happy and excited. You should be—trust me!

This step is crucial. You need to understand who you are. You can create a sketch of the new, stronger, and super-motivated you in just a few seconds. If your choices should change—we all change, and so do our plans—make sure you redefine yourself again.

A brief example: I have a friend who is an excellent hairdresser. However, her business wasn't that great. Do you know why? It's simple. She would define herself as a hairdresser, not an entrepreneur or business owner. All she had to do was think of herself as an entrepreneur that also has fantastic hairdressing skills. She had to create a new definition of herself, a definition of a successful businesswoman, not just passionate hairdresser. Her new definition motivated her to spend more time with other business owners and learn from them. She learned how to leave her comfort zone.

Now that you are all "redefined" and your mindset is ready after having an excellent workout, it's time to dive into the next step.

Chapter 4
Step 4 – Redefine Your Goals, Spice It Up, Make It Juicy, and Get Super Excited for What Is Just About to Happen

There are so many people out there who want to be successful with their goals. They worked hard to eradicate negative thinking and are initially motivated to take action, but they fail miserably because they miss out on a critical detail. That detail is knowing EXACTLY what you want, why you want it, and how it will help you improve specific areas or all areas of your life.

If your goal is to make more money, lose more weight, be more successful, or travel more, guess what—you are not doing yourself a great favor. You need to know exactly what you want. It's like looking for a particular kind of product or buying a car. You just need to know what you want and be as precise and accurate as possible.

You have probably heard of the SMART rule.

It basically means that your goals need to be:

- Specific

- Measurable

- Attainable

- Realistic

- have a Timeline

If you ignore the SMART rule, you are just dreaming. Dreams are awesome and motivate us. However, we need to turn dreams into smaller, doable goals and take action on them. If you don't have a plan, you don't have a goal, and it's still a dream and wishful thinking.

I also believe in flexibility. Sometimes you may change your goals and plan for life. This may be because you have found something even better or have new opportunities cropping up. It's okay to modify and redefine your goals. The most important thing is to...

Start writing your goals down. Start planning. Make sure you have your goals for this year, this month, this week, and today. This will light your motivational fire.

I am a big fan of holistic medicine, and its basic concept is that everyone is different. This is why people may develop different ways of writing down and planning their goals.

What I have learned is that the most important thing is just to keep doing it because eventually, you will know what works for you and what doesn't. In this step, I will share with you what I do daily, weekly, and monthly and how it helps me. Take what you like and reject the rest. I am sure that as soon as you get started, you will develop your unique way. Everyone is special and unique. I encourage you to share Your Unique Way with other readers. The review section of this book is an excellent place to share your thoughts. Remember that creating your unique way may take some time. Again, I encourage you to get into a habit of writing your goals down. It's non-negotiable.

According to many motivational speakers, for example, Tony Robbins, less than 5 percent of our population writes their goals down. Less than 5 percent! How sad is that?

Most of those people usually write their goals down only once a year, usually around New Years. Apparently, only 1 percent of our population writes their goals daily. It blew my mind when I heard that. This fact has motivated me to get into the small percentage of people who write their goals down daily, sometimes even twice a day. It's a potent tool, not only for your subconscious mind but as a general positive reminder.

When you write your goals down every day, it helps you overcome pain and rejection, and trust me; these will also appear on your way to success. When you write your goals down, you are entirely focused on what you want and where you are going as opposed to what other people want, what is happening, and where you are coming from. You escape from being reactive, and you create a solid, proactive foundation.

Let's go through the process together:

1. Write down a specific goal.

If you want to lose weight, write down exactly how much weight you want to lose and make sure you have a realistic deadline. Include a short description of how you will look. For example: "I have a sexy, fit body, and I can wear what I want. I look like a fitness instructor." Make it juicy and precise!

If you want abundance, write down exactly how much money a month you want to make. Again, have a deadline. Finally, come up with a short description of your desired result: "I travel to exotic locations at least twice a year. I have my own company, and I hire a team of brilliant individuals. My business is growing, and I change the world. I have managed to buy my dream house with cash, and I live an awesome lifestyle." Again, make it juicy!

Remember, these are just examples. Use them as a template to write down your goals.

Here is the best language to write down your goals:

I will easily [add your specific goal] by [specific date], and I will love the process of achieving this goal because...

2.Come up with all of the WHYs. How does achieving your goal, or at least making some progress toward it, change your life?

I have noticed that many people fail with their goals and moving forward to achieve more because they only have one WHY behind their desired outcomes. I believe that one is not enough. Again, you really need to make it juicy! When creating my first Udemy course, I actually came up with 26 reasons why. I even included how going through the actual process of creating a course would help me overcome the fear of public speaking and how I could become a better person because of it. I asked myself these questions:

-How can achieving my goal (in that case, creating my first online course) help me transform all areas of my life?

-How can going through the actual process of achieving this goal help me transform all areas of my life?

You see, it's not only about the final result. It's also about embracing the process of getting closer to desired outcome. The process is always full of surprise gifts waiting for you!

Now please go ahead and do the same. Think about the process as well as the final result and how they will change your life. Even small changes and lessons count. As soon as you have more than five reasons to do something, you will get super excited.

Let me give you an example. Let's say that a person wants to make more money, so they are committed to creating products or services. They may just say, "Oh yeah, when I achieve that goal, I will be making this amount of money a month."

OK, I get it. That's not bad, and it's specific. However, it could be juicier, maybe spicier. It would be much better to say:

Thanks to achieving this goal, I will have enough money to eat healthy, organic food and hire a personal trainer. I will be able to buy the clothes I want. I will be able to go on a family vacation every three months.

If you have kids, you could also say something like: I will be able to provide for my family and spend more time with them.

The bottom line is this: If you have financial goals, make sure that you write down how achieving your goals (and not even achieving but also going through the process of completing them) will help you positively impact other areas of your life (health, social life, and family).

The same thing goes the other way around. If you have a health and fitness goal, your *whys* could also relate to your wealth. For example: *When I lose weight and take care of my health, I will have more energy to focus on my career and make more money as a result.*

My tip:

It's all interconnected. Don't separate one area of your life from another. Don't wait to achieve financial success to start taking care of your health. To me, my health and fitness goals are as important as my business goals. I need a healthy body and focused mind. Besides, I am a wellness coach, and I am proud to say that I practice what I preach. Even when I get a bit off track, I always find a way get up, brush myself off, and move forward again.

2.Now, close your eyes and visualize yourself once the goal is achieved. Focus on your feelings and emotions. Open your eyes, grab your journal, and write down a few sentences. For example:

> *- I am working out in a gym, looking amazing, and people ask me if I am a fitness coach.*

> *- I am getting pampered in a spa in the Bahamas.*

> *- I have a book of my authorship in my hands, and I sign it for other people.*

> *- I lie on the beach, and I am proud of the healthy body I have created.*

> Remember—keep it juicy!

Going through the process mentioned above will keep you excited. All you need to do now is to take action. You have two choices:

1.Join the high percentage of people who never bother to define their goal or write it down.

2.Enter the small percentage of individuals who invest their time in writing down their goals, as well as all the *whys* behind them, who are successful.

Which pill have you chosen to take?

The blue one? Good job! Now, let's move on.

Realistic vs. Unrealistic

There is an additional, advanced strategy that you may find helpful. Let's get back to the SMART rule. It says that your goals need to be realistic. Yes, I agree, your short-term goals should be realistic. However, I am also a dreamer. I believe that you can be a realistic dreamer as well. I use dreams to motivate me to take even more action to overcome myself, leave my comfort zone and push myself.

Here's a recommended exercise you can try:

Grab your journal and write down a few long-term goals that you still have no idea how you will achieve. So what? We all need dreams in the form of long-term goals. What inspires you? Also, remember that you need to expand your mindset. Here is how you should write down your long-term, UNREALISTIC goals. They will remind you where you're going.

Examples of long-term and unrealistic goals (they will be your reality sooner than you can imagine):

- I have two successful global companies. I am so grateful for that!

- I live in a mansion/penthouse that I bought with cash. I am extremely grateful that I could make it happen.

- I am a mother/father of four children and I feel so blessed.

- I have a foundation, and I help people in third-world countries. I feel privileged to change the world.

- I have a swimming pool and private gym.

- I travel abroad five times a year or more.

Some people say that all your goals must be realistic, and again, I agree. Your short-term goals must be realistic. However, by defining your long-term goals, even if they are still dreams and a bit blurred, you create your ultimate VISION.

You need to have a VISION. Vision means a passion for life. All successful people had their vision even if they had no idea how they would achieve it and make it a reality.

Here is the full process I go through every morning and again every evening before I go to sleep.

- I come up with at least one long-term goal. I write it in present tense, and I express my gratitude, feeling it with every cell of my body as if I have already achieved it.
- After that, I usually feel excited, and so I write down my top three monthly goals (I will easily _____ by the end of _____, and I will love the process of achieving this goal).
- Then, I relocate my attention specifically on this week and my goals for the present.
- Finally, I finish off by planning my day if it's morning, or if it's the evening, giving myself an honest review of what I could have done better and also what went amazingly well. It's good to pat yourself on the back.

Now it's your turn! Start writing. Yes, you are writing and creating the Book of Your Life!

What we have learned in this chapter:

- Make sure you always write your goals down. Use the SMART method for your short-term goals. Create a habit of writing your goals down daily!

- Always come up with as many whys as you possibly can. Picture how your life will change after achieving your goal and what you will learn in the process of completing it. Remember that the more you achieve, the stronger you get and the easier it gets for you to achieve even more!

- Writing your goals down daily or even twice a day will automatically make you join the elite ranks of doers and achievers. Don't use excuses like "I don't have time." You can always find five minutes in the morning and five in the evening. You can even do it on your lunch break!

- Make sure that you have some long-term goals and a vision, even if, for the time being, it's beyond your reach. Personally, I want to buy my own house with cash, no mortgages. I want a swimming pool in my house. That is currently a bit far away, but it motivates me to take action on my short-term goals which will eventually help me get there.

– If your goal is to have a nice family life, create a goal like, for example, having a wife or a husband and a bunch of kids. Even if for the time being you don't have a partner and are still looking for your soulmate, you can still dream. Your ultimate vision will help you become stronger and overcome obstacles. Even if you go through the pain of relationship breakups, your vision will help you move forward.

– When writing down your long-term goals and your vision, always use the present tense and express as much gratitude as you possibly can.

Final tips:

- Be relaxed and confident about your goals. You know that you deserve the best. Forget about self-doubt and fear. If they ever appear in your mind, just snuff them out by taking your journal and writing down your vision and goals. Focus on where you are going, not where you're coming from.

Chapter 5
Step 5 – Take Massive Action and Create as Many Positive Reminders as You Can Possibly Think Of

OK, my friend. Now you are in the right mindset, you have your goals and vision, and you know exactly what you want, why you want it, and how it can transform your life. I want to congratulate you. You have managed to complete the first part of the journey, the part that, in my personal opinion, is the most crucial in the whole process I describe in this program.

Now, it's time for you to take action. You need to make sure that you have the right information and plan. Since this is a general mindset transformation book, it will not go into detail on specific how-tos of specific goals, for example, fitness, weight loss, or starting a business. I believe that as soon as you get 100 percent committed to your goal, you will find your plan and your way.

68

Here are my general tips:

- When looking for specific how-to and information to follow to achieve your goal, make sure you don't go overboard. Too much information can turn into a bad thing. Focus is the key. For example, when I decided to create my first Udemy course, I only picked up two how-to courses that were created by extremely successful Udemy teachers. I have seen some people take 20 different courses or more, but they still haven't taken action. Too much information can take your motivation away and make you feel paralyzed.

- I believe it's vital to have a good teacher, instructor, coach, mentor, or whatever you want to call it. You can either pick up their course, program, or book, attend their seminar, or hire them as a personal coach. The last option can be pretty expensive. This is why I am a big believer in books, courses, and programs. The key point is to have someone you can follow. Someone who has walked the path before you. Make sure you get quality advice and aren't being scammed. Again, you need to learn from someone who has already achieved what you want to.

- After picking one particular program or a method, follow through and get committed to it 100 percent.

You need to see if it works for you. For example, I see that many people who want to lose weight or get healthy in general pick up way too many diets or programs. One week they go Paleo, then they go vegan, and then they ponder something else. Of course, I am not saying that you should blindly follow through, even if the given information does not work for you. Usually, a certain amount of patience and effort is required. Again, I am just giving you some general mindset and motivational tips on how to make sure you have the right information so that you can take meaningful and purposeful action and get good results.

-Avoid doing and figuring out how to do things on your own. If you can find someone who has achieved success in whatever it is that you want, simply follow their methods and strategies. There is no point in reinventing the wheel. At the same time, allow yourself some degree of flexibility if needed.

-Like I said before, too much information can be bad for your overall focus and motivation. For example, I have a friend who has been struggling to have a successful online business, but instead of just sticking to one thing, she keeps jumping all over the place. She subscribes to 50 different newsletters, buys 15 different courses (that she does not have time to go through), and instead of focusing on one business model, she goes from one thing to another. Again, focus on one thing. When that's done, or if it's not working for you, then move on to the next thing. But don't give up straight away because something doesn't work. Of course, use your intuition. If something is not working for you, move on to something new. This can be applied to all areas of life: health, finances, career, and even relationships. You need some level of flexibility as well as patience and what I call "being a stubborn mule." But don't do it too much. Sometimes, it may be time to quit and focus on something different.

Now that you have a plan and information to rely on, you need to remodel and adapt your current lifestyle. In other words, everything should be moving around you and your goal, keeping you extremely motivated at the same time. If your goal is to get super fit and ripped, and you want to be working out in a gym six times a week, you need a certain amount of planning and dedication. Think of possible obstacles and temptations and how to overcome them. When do you need to get up? How much time a day do you need to spend on your workouts and their preparation? Where are you going to get that extra time? Maybe cutting down on Facebook and instant messaging? Or maybe cooking in batches or using a crockpot so that you spend less time cooking but always have delicious and nutritious meals that support your goals?

The same applies to your business or career. If your goal is to create a brand, be prepared to work more than you usually do. It's not going to be forever; it's only going to be temporary. Whatever it is that you want, you need to understand that there will be some sacrifice. Again, what time are you going to get up every day to make it happen?

If you want to be successful, you need to accept the fact that there will be sacrifices. For example, in my case, it was my social life. I wanted to focus on my career and business goals, and I would spend long hours studying, creating my brand, and learning more about business. I had to get up early and keep doing what I was doing. I also worked on weekends, and I still do that pretty often. But now it's no longer a sacrifice for me. I do it because I choose to and because it is my passion.

So do you. The word "sacrifice" may evoke some negative feelings. I suggest you start using the verb "choose" instead.

For example:

- I choose to work on my business and gain financial freedom for my family.

- I choose to work on my body and look like a fitness model.

- I choose to eat a healthy diet and create more energy and zest for life.

Every day when you get up, I want you to come up with three things that you CHOOSE to do that day. Only three. They can be small. Maybe you don't have time to go to the gym. But you can still choose to:

- Have a wheat grass drink;

- Do a 15-minute workout while playing your favorite music;

- Meditate for 5 minutes and refresh yourself with some essential oils.

If you focus on your career or business, you can choose to read books or articles that will help you achieve your goals.

Even 15 minutes a day spent reading can help you. If time is an issue, grab some audiobooks. What else do you have to do when you drive, commute to work, shop, or clean? Audiobooks are like free college. You can learn a lot while spending almost nothing. Making sure that you always stick to your goal and create plans B, C, and D in case something crops up, or you don't have time. These techniques will help you keep more motivated. Why? Because you will be in motion!

Remember: What you choose to do today creates your tomorrow. It's always those little things.

The connection between the Law of Action and the Law of Attraction

I very often get asked about the Law of Attraction since I believe in working on your inner energy. I believe that it works and can help you achieve your goals.

However—and this is a very big however—I am not saying that you can just sit down and visualize your future and it will all come true. I also believe in what I call the Law of Action. Even if you analyze the teachers from the book *The Secret*, they all took action in their own way, and they all had entrepreneurial projects going on.

In my opinion, to succeed, you need a certain balance between the Law of Attraction and the Law of Action. You can utilize the Law of Attraction to feel good and positive about your goals. I think that it can also be a great motivator. I love vision boards and similar stuff. However, don't forget to take action!

I also think that if you just stick to the Law of Action but neglect the Law of Attraction, you end up taking too much action. This can make you feel negative or insecure; your success may be delayed or halted completely.

You need to take action from the place of confidence, abundance, happiness, and security. If you take action from the point of anger, impatience, frustration, and self-doubt, you may end up putting in lots of hard work but not seeing the results. My tip for you: Don't neglect your inner energy. Try to maintain the positive attitude. Whenever you feel like negativity is taking over you, get back to the previous steps of this program. Write down your goals and get excited about them again. Cultivate gratitude for your past and future achievements.

What's the right proportion between Action and Attraction? Well, there is no definite rule. Ask yourself; it depends on how you feel. One thing is sure, if you are not getting the results you want, it's because of one (or all) of the following:

- You don't work hard enough.
- You don't work smart enough.
- Your strategy does not work.
- You neglected the Law of Attraction and did not get rid of negative feelings that are stopping you from achieving success.
- You are not taking massive action; what you're doing is not enough.

My favorite motivators that help me embrace both the Law of Attraction as well as the Law of Action:

1.Create vision boards. Of course, they will not do the work for you but think of them as positive reminders and motivators. I have different vision boards for various areas of my life: health, fitness, and lifestyle. And it works! My fitness vision board motivates me to work out every day. Just because I see it every day! Now I do short workouts even in my office because I know they help me work better and be more productive. Guess what kind of a vision board I have in my kitchen. You guessed it—it's full of healthy recipes! Go online and look for pictures that motivate and inspire you. Print them out or get them professionally printed. Then put them in different categories. Have your ideal lifestyle vision board, your health and fitness vision board, and even your super rich vision board! They will help you focus and take action, even if you have a bad day.

2.Listen to motivational and inspirational podcasts and videos every day. Yes, every day! Most people would say that this is only necessary when you feel down or not motivated at all, but I would say that you should listen to them even if you feel good about your goals. You can always feel better. Pick up podcasters or YouTubers that you resonate with. What your friend may find inspiring may not be that inspiring for you and vice versa. After all, everyone is different. With podcasts and other audio programs, you can not only take advantage of your cleaning, driving, or walking times when your brain is usually filled with nothing, but you can also feed your mind with positive messages and knowledge. This is what I call positive brainwashing.

Listening to motivational podcasts will also help you feel stronger if you are exposed to negative people and environments.

3.PIN method.

PIN method is something I came up with in one of my old blog posts, and so far I have been getting very positive feedback about it. It stands for positive, inspiration, and negative. It's a short exercise that I suggest you go through now so that you can condition your mind for success and keep your motivation on fire.

-P stands for POSITIVE

How will achieving your goals or at least making progress toward them change your life? You have already answered this question in the precious chapters but do it again. Think of as many positive things as you can.

-I stands for INSPIRATION

How will achieving your goal and taking action toward it inspire those around you? Think about how you will become a role model for other people. Your actions and decisions can encourage someone and help them transform their lives. There is someone out there feeling sad or depressed, and your positive and motivational lifestyle can help them. This is your responsibility now. You can't chicken out!

-N stands for NEGATIVE

According to Tony Robbins, humans will do more to avoid pain rather than to gain pleasure. Try to come up with as many negative things that can happen to you if you don't take action now. Is quitting an answer? Or are you willing to do whatever it takes to avoid unnecessary pain? What is it that you want to avoid at all costs? An unhealthy body and no energy, no ability to live the life that you want, or a job you hate and hardly make a living doing? Remember that your mind is stronger than you believe. It will help you avoid pain and get wherever you want, but you need to learn to control and operate it. The more you do it, the easier it gets. It's just like learning to drive, playing a new instrument, or practicing new sports.

The bottom line is that you need to take action. If you don't, you will move quite a few steps backward, and from there, there is only the World of Excuses and bitterness. Nope, we don't want to be there, right?

In this chapter, we have learned how to:

- Utilize the Law of Attraction and the Law of Action without going overboard with either of them;

- Create positive reminders and motivators;

- Use positive and negative conditioning to achieve your goals and stay motivated;

- Make sure you have the right amount of information that you can stick to and rely on in order to achieve your goals faster.

Chapter 6
Step 6 – How to Stick to Your Plan, Keep Going and Never Give Up; Overcome Obstacles and Learn How to Deal with Haters

If I were to tell you that success is always easy, I would be lying to you. Besides, I believe that preparation is key. Achieving your goals is like a journey, and there might always be something cropping up. Sometimes that "something" may even get you off track if you don't know how to prepare yourself.

If you want to keep your motivation at the highest levels, you must accept these facts:

- There will be obstacles. Life is not a bed of roses.
- There will be days when you "don't feel like it" or just feel under the weather for some reason. You will still need to move forward and be committed.

- There might be criticism, and some people may even attack you for your drive for success. Strangely enough, some people don't like to see other individuals who take action and create their dreams lives. You will need to learn how to use criticism to your advantage to either improve your work or strengthen your emotional muscles and move forward.

- Some of your strategies may not work, so you may be forced to go a few steps backward to move forward again. Think about it as losing your compass on your way. You simply have to go back and find it.

- You may realize that it takes a bit longer to achieve your goals. Again, remember that you need to be flexible. If you require more time to achieve your goal, then take more time. It's better to take more time and get better results than to rush and get less-than-stellar results, right?

You already know that perfection does not exist. It's all about progress. But you see, obstacles make us stronger and help us make progress, even if we need to put more time and effort into achieving our goals!

Whenever you are facing a challenge, learn what you can get from it. Use it to your advantage. You need to keep your motivation high. This is why I recommend that you:

-Go through the list of all your *whys*—the list you wrote down before you got started on your work. Go through the whole list again. Get your passion back and focus on your vision.

-Pick up your journal and create positive affirmations. It will help you calm down chaotic thoughts and turn negative into positive.

-Pick up an inspirational story, whether it's a book, podcast, or video. You will realize you are not alone. Success is not easy; it is a process. Be patient. Keep going. Never give up.

Create a Positive Environment

I think it's crucial to make sure that those around you support you. Even if their goals are different than yours or they have different lifestyle choices, if you feel like there is someone out there who believes in you, it can empower you and put you back on track.

From my experience, I know it can be hard to make all the people around you understand what you're doing. If you want to become an entrepreneur and those around you choose to have jobs and think that what you're doing is weird (or the other way around), you may find it harder to stick to your business creation. If, however, they respect your choices, even if their own decisions are different, it's a different story.

Respect others and ask them to do the same for you.

Don't get angry or frustrated if those around you choose a different lifestyle than your own. Again, people make different choices, and everyone is on a different journey. Stop judging others, and you will see that others will stop judging you. I had to learn this the hard way.

For example, when I first started on my healthy lifestyle, I would go around and preach to all my friends. I would tell them to eat healthily, go to the gym, or quit smoking. Guess what. I finally realized I was a bit too judgmental. There is a difference between giving advice when it's needed and going overboard. Many people around me would not respect or support my new choices, and I would not respect theirs. It wasn't until I chilled out a bit and used it as a motivator that I started to gain respect. I decided to get more committed to my healthy lifestyle to get more visible results. Ever since I transformed my body, many of my friends started to ask me what I did and if I had any "coaching slots" available for them.

Lesson learned: If those around you don't understand your current lifestyle choices and goals, don't take it personally. Everyone is on a different journey. Respect their way and passionately stick to yours. This is your new motivator. You need to get better results to inspire those around you.

Aside from that, I recommend you start joining mastermind groups. You need to make friends with people who are on a similar journey and understand your mindset. Some of them may be your accountability buddies. You can create your offline mastermind group locally by using meetup.com, or you can look for online groups on Facebook and Google+. Don't go overboard. There is no reason to join dozens of groups.

If you want to lose weight and stick to a particular diet (such as Paleo, vegan, or alkaline), try to find people with the same goals. Their energy will help you get there faster. Besides, it's exciting! Your journey will help you make more incredible connections, and many of them will be global connections! The internet is such a great invention!

Finally, about criticism. Don't fear it; embrace it!

All successful people have their haters, so don't worry if you have them, too.

I am like a broken record with that. I'm sure you agree by now.

You see, what we have in common is that we admire successful people, and we use their success story as motivation and inspiration. But not all the people in the world think that way. It's not their fault. It's just that they don't know how to use someone's success to their advantage, they have limiting beliefs, or they got hurt and turned into haters. Be empathic toward them, and try to send them good, positive energy.

Some people learn how to learn from successful people whereas others only learn how to hate them. Again, never pay back with hate.

Also, be open to constructive criticism and feedback. Some people just want to help you. Don't take all the criticism personally. Finally, everyone has the right not to like something. Some people may not like what you're doing, but it doesn't mean they hate you.

Remember, everyone is different, and everyone makes different choices.

I know that some people will like this book, and they will resonate with me. Some people will not like this book even if they like me. Some people will not like me or this book because, for some reason, it's not for them. The fact that they don't like something does not make them haters. Everyone has different tastes.

Now you are prepared to move forward. This is the key to success!

In this chapter, you have learned how to:

- Deal with haters and criticism and utilize them as an asset;
- Keep going even if you are frustrated;
- Turn negative into positive;
- Get your passion back in place;
- Create positive environments that keep your motivation and focus high;
- Stay motivated even if those around you are making different lifestyle choices.

Chapter 7
Step 7 – Get Ready to Achieve More. Think as an Achiever and Action-Taker

Congratulations! You are now ready to crush it with your goals. You are confident and know what to do even when pain and rejection crop up on your way to success.

In this chapter, I want to push you to achieve more. Once you have been through this process, you can go through it all over again. Don't just stop. You need to carry on. I understand that sometimes you need to relax and slow down to supercharge your batteries, but don't forget about your vision and long-term goals.

Now it's time to repeat the process with your new goals. At the same time, you need to remember that motivation is especially important at the beginning of your journey. Then, you need to focus on creating your powerful success habits and motivational rituals. These may include:

- Journaling every day—non-negotiable. You are successful, and this is what all successful people do. It's just who you are!
- Creating more vision boards and dreaming. You need to expand your mindset. There are so many awesome things waiting for you. You just need to take more action to get them.
- Reading books on success and successful people who inspire you.
- Be an active member of your local mastermind group and interact with like-minded individuals.
- Make sure you always have your daily, weekly, monthly, and yearly goals specified, but of course, allow some level of flexibility.
- Be HUNGRY for success! You can never be successful enough!

You now know that achieving your goals and staying motivated is about understanding the difference between the process and result. I am sure that now you know that success is never an event that just happens. There is always work, effort, time, vision, passion, and perseverance, and all of these are managed by the powerful motivation.

As soon as you focus on the process and embrace the fact that it's not only about achieving your final goal but also about enjoying the journey, you will see that you will not feel scared to achieve more. You will understand that you want to live your life by your design and that you want to live to your full potential. You will feel how every step of your journey makes you stronger and more motivated.

There is always a process to go through, and this book taught you the basic mindset behind it. There are no shortcuts. It takes time and effort to transform your body and create more vibrant health. It takes time and effort to study and learn new things. It takes time and effort to create a brand and start a business just like it takes time and effort to create a healthy lifestyle. But lighting our motivational fires can do incredible things in our lives and make us so much happier!

We were born to create and transform not only our lives but also those of others. We are not here to sit around and complain. Laziness is a killer. Creativity and action backed up by inner motivation are game-changers.

Shortcuts don't exist. Let's say a person wants to lose weight, and they decide to get a liposuction procedure. They get the result, of course, but since they haven't been through the process of learning how to eat healthy, figuring out what diet works for them, and how to work out, they will put the weight right back on. If, however, a person masters the process, they can use it all over again to master other areas of their life. The mindset is always the same.

You need to stay active. Have new goals. Go higher. These are the words of wisdom from my late grandfather. He survived hard times of the Second World War and was even in a German work camp. He had to develop mental toughness, and at the same time, gratitude. I think this is the key to success. This is why, when I wrote my first book, I knew I had to carry on. I knew I had to climb higher. I want my granddad to be proud of me. He managed to achieve a lot even in the times of hardship and political turmoil. So could my other granddad and grandmas. Their lives were not easy, but they still found a way to make it.

This is why I believe that there is nothing I can complain about. All I need to do is be grateful for what I have, work on my body, mind, and spirit, and move forward. This is my personal motivator. What are yours? Is there anyone in your family you want to make proud of you? Your actions and achievements will surely make them proud. Even if they are not here physically to see your progress, they can feel it and know it.

Now it's time for you to carry on. The DEAL is your dream life.

Keep doing and inspiring. Write your words of wisdom using the pen of action. It will help you to inspire other people. This will also be your motivator.

Free 5 Day Motivation Challenge + Free Audio Download

I want you to succeed with this book. For that to happen, you need to consolidate and practice what you have just learned.

This is why I would like to offer you a free 5-day motivation challenge:

www.LifestyleDesignSuccess.com/motivation

Every day, you will receive a super useful motivational tip to make sure you keep on track. I will also spoil you with some bonus motivational audios and videos (so that you know who's talking to you).

You will be able to keep in touch with me via email and ask me questions.

Why do I do this?

I used to struggle with motivation as well. But by helping other people get and stay motivated, I also help myself keep on track!

Sign up for free here.

Let's do this!

Join the free challenge and grab your free audio at:

www.lifestyledesignsuccess.com/motivation

Conclusion – Success is Yours. Just Take It!

Thanks again for taking an interest in my book. I hope that you enjoyed it and that I was able to motivate you.

We are all different and may have different goals, but the process of achieving them and making them reality is always the same. It all comes down to working on your mindset, making friends with your emotions and feelings, and getting committed to success.

Is there any motivational tip that inspired you in particular?

If so, please post a short review on Amazon and let me know.

It's you I am writing for, and I would love to hear from you. Believe it or not, whenever I get a new review, I read it all over again, and I dance around like a little kid. This is how happy and excited I get!

Thanks again for picking up this book. Take positive and meaningful action and get amazing results. I believe in you!

And don't forget to enjoy the journey. It's the journey that makes us stronger and motivated us to take more action.

Let's connect:

My blog: www.LifestyleDesignSuccess.com

(entrepreneurship, motivation, lifestyle design)

Follow me on Social Media, let's keep in touch:

YT: www.LifestyleDesignSuccess.com/youtube

FB: www.facebook.com/lifestyledesignsuccess

IG: www.instagram.com/lifestyledesignsuccess

Made in the USA
Middletown, DE
17 February 2018